Getting Your Great Ideas Rolling
(in an Uphill World)

AWAKE
at the
WHEEL

MITCHELL LEWIS DITKOFF

MORGAN JAMES PUBLISHING • NEW YORK

Copyright ©2008 Mitchell Lewis Ditkoff

Library of Congress Control Number 2007935671

ISBN: 978-1-60037-295-7 (Paperback)
ISBN: 978-1-60037-296-4 (Hardcover)

Published by:

MORGAN · JAMES™
THE ENTREPRENEURIAL PUBLISHER
www.morganjamespublishing.com

Morgan James Publishing, LLC
1225 Franklin Ave Ste 32
Garden City, NY 11530-1693
Toll Free 800-485-4943
www.MorganJamesPublishing.com

Cover/Interior Design by:
Rachel Campbell
rachel@r2cdesign.com

Habitat for Humanity®
Peninsula Building Partner

"Whatever you can do,
or dream you can, begin it.
Boldness has genius, power
and magic in it."
— Goethe

ADVANCED PRAISE FOR AWAKE AT THE WHEEL

"*A superb catalyst* for anyone with the urge to bring their best ideas into reality."
— *Tim Gallwey, Author of* Inner Game of Tennis *and* Inner Game of Work

"Og may have invented the wheel, but Mitch Ditkoff has created a GPS for the innovation process. *Awake at the Wheel* is a witty and inspiring roadmap for the journey from ideas to invention!"
— *Donna Fenn, Author,* Alpha Dogs: How Your Small Business Can Become a Leader of the Pack

"This easy to read allegory reinvents and refreshes our thinking about what it takes to move from inspiration to actualization. I highly recommend Mitch's deep thinking to all who would bring their Big Ideas into the harsh and resistant Real World."
— *Dr. Barry Gruenberg, Director of Leadership Development, Microsoft Corporation*

"A highly accessible alchemist's stone for aspiring innovators."
— *Joyce Wycoff, Co-founder of Innovation Network, President of ThinkSmart Learning Systems*

"*Awake at the Wheel* illuminates! It's the perfect book for those of us who have felt the excitement of the 'aha' moment only to experience the frustration that comes when no one sees the brilliant light bulb above our head. Mitch Ditkoff takes us on an engaging journey that re-imagines how to turn an idea into great success and makes it suddenly seem easy."

— *Melinda McLaughlin, SVP, A&E Television Networks*

"Entertaining and inspiring."

— *Chuck Frey, Founder, Innovation Tools*

"Cheese, Fish and Peacocks are so last century when Og (aka Mitch Ditkoff) is at the wheel! *Awake at the Wheel* packs so much into such a deceptively whimsical story that it comes together in a "perfect storm" of innovation that speaks to everyone. If you need to get your creative juices flowing (or your team's), read this book immediately."

— *Debbie Weathers, Organizational Learning, Merck*

"Want to jump start your creative self? *Awake at the Wheel* is a delightful story that engages, entertains, and elevates your thinking about innovation."

— *Leslie Yerkes, Author,* Fun Works: Creating Places Where People Love to Work

"A light-hearted tour through the world of ideas: how to let them in, nourish them, and manifest them to a waiting world. Mitch (and Og) are here to help you do as you dream.*"*

– Erika Andersen, Founder of Proteus International and
author of Growing Great Employees

"In *Awake at the Wheel*, Mitch Ditkoff takes storytelling to new levels of entertainment, practicality, and wisdom. This little tome is packed with powerful lessons, direction, and advice for anyone attempting to turn their ideas into reality."

– Farrell Reynolds, Former Director of Sales, Turner Broadcasting

"Through an artful and engaging use of story, metaphor, and a practical toolkit, *Awake at the Wheel* provides a very accessible, yet thoroughly original guide about what it takes to create breakthroughs, from idea generation to execution. Mitch Ditkoff is an educator who embodies his message completely – by teaching about innovation innovatively."

– Michael A. Chavez Jr., Managing Director, Duke Corporate Education

"Go ahead and 'hug' your employees by giving them *Awake at the Wheel* and creating a company culture that fosters, develops, and celebrates the best of their ideas!"

– Jack Mitchell, Author of Hug Your Customers *and* Hug Your People

"A fun fable from the past with profound implications for the future. For those who think BIG IDEAS, peek inside for the most powerful business tools I've found."

— Joe Belinsky, Professor, Kent State University

"A fantastic little book on ideas."

— Rick Frishman, President, Planned TV Arts and Co-Author of Author 101

"This amusing, playful book describes with uncanny familiarity The Creative Person's Journey. If you've ever had an idea you wanted to bring into being, you'll love *Awake at the Wheel*!"

— David Garfinkel, Founder, World Copywriting Institute and Author of Advertising Headlines That Make You Rich

"Anyone who's ever taken a shower has had a great idea. Unfortunately, most ideas vaporize in the shower along with the steam. Awake at the Wheel shows how to nurture great ideas and turn them into reality. This unique and playful book has a serious message: Ideas are gifts deserving of our respect. That means knowing how to cultivate and manifest them. Read *Awake at the Wheel*, and don't let your next great idea get away!"

— Larry Pinci & Phil Glosserman, Authors of Sell the Feeling: The 6-Step System that Drives People to Do Business with You

"Nothing is as powerful as an idea whose time has come. The time has come for this book and Mitchell Ditkoff has put it into words. He has done a masterful job."

— *Jay Conrad Levinson, The Father of Guerrilla Marketing,*
Author, "Guerrilla Marketing" series of books
with over 15 million sold; now in 43 languages

"There are over six billion brains thinking on earth at this moment. If just a tiny fraction of those brains were exposed to *Awake at the Wheel*.....the world would be alot easier for all of us to enjoy. Everybody has the potential to be creative and make an impact. We just need to spark our brain into action. Mitchell Ditkoff provides a great tool to make that spark happen."

— *Neil Shulman MD, Author and Associate Producer* Doc Hollywood

TABLE OF CONTENTS

ACKNOWLEDGMENTS

Awake at the Wheel would not exist without the loving support of many wonderful people in my life. My heartfelt thanks to all of them. • My teacher, Prem Rawat (aka Maharaji), for showing me the timeless place beyond ideas • Barney and Sylvia for bringing me into the world • Evelyne for all her love and support • Jesse and Mimi for being such awesome kids • Steve Ornstein for being my Ugh • Val Vadeboncoeur for his sense of humor • Ron Brent for his timeless perspective • Scott Cronin for his soulful friendship • Erika Andersen for her clarity • Nancy Seroka for taking care of business • Tim Moore for his generosity of spirit • Carl Frankel, Barbara Bash, Hudson Talbott, and Pat Anderson for their feedback and encouragement • Steve McHugh for co-founding Idea Champions • Michael Schacker for Ingenuity Bank • Bill Shockley for opening doors • Jon Lloyd for his kindness • Bill Ross for his idea for a better ending • Rachel Campbell for her book design • David Hancock, Wes Taylor, Margo Toulouse, and all the wonderful people at Morgan James Publishing for getting this book into your hands.

WHAT'S THE BIG IDEA?

This is a book about ideas. *Your* ideas. *Where* they come from. *Why* you get them. And *how* to radically increase your chances of manifesting them – regardless of the seeming obstacles in your way. But even more importantly, it's a book about the *creative act* – that mysterious process out of which new ideas make their appearance in the world.

I wrote this book because I had to. It was bursting in me to be born. Having spent the past 20 years of my life designing and leading creative thinking sessions for a wide variety of corporations, I decided it was time to distill what I had learned down to its irreducible core. My intention? To spark a renaissance of life-changing ideas – ideas that will not only improve *your* life but the lives of people everywhere.

Ultimately, *everything begins with an idea*. Whether you're in business, school, jail, or debt, that's how it all gets rolling. First there's the idea, then there's the manifestation of the idea – assuming, of course, that the person *with* the idea has their act together. If you have any doubt, take a look around you. Everything you see began as an idea: the microchip, the chocolate chip, the fishing net, the internet, the company you work for, and the company you keep. All of it. Everything. Even the universe, some say, began as an idea in the mind of the Creator.

Well then, if it all begins with an idea, where in the world do ideas come from?

There are two schools of thought on this subject. The first ascribes the origin of ideas to the efforts of inspired individuals who conjure them up through a series of spontaneously occurring or purposeful mental processes. The second school of thought ascribes the appearance of ideas to a transcendent force, a.k.a. the "Collective Unconscious," the "Platonic Realm," the "Muse," or the "Mind of God." According to this perspective, ideas are not created, but already exist – becoming accessible to human beings who have tuned themselves enough to be able to *receive* them.

The first approach is usually considered Western, with a strong bias towards *thinking,* and is best summarized by Rene Descartes' "I think therefore I am" maxim. Most business people subscribe to this approach, as it gives great weight to the power of the intellect. The second approach is usually considered Eastern, with a strong bias towards *feeling,* and is best summarized by the opposite of the Cartesian view: *"I am therefore, I think."* Most artists and "creative types" are associated with this approach, with its focus on *intuitive knowing*. Both approaches are valid. Both are effective. And both are used at different times by all of us, depending on our mood, circumstances, and conditioning.

No matter what our preferred approach, however, the challenge remains the same for all of us: *how to honor, develop, and manifest our ideas*. This is a challenge made increasingly more difficult these days by the fact that, somehow, ideas have gotten a bad rap. If you have one, chances are good that you apologize before talking about it with some variation of "Uh…er…*it's just an idea.*" Most of us, in fact, have made a habit of discounting ideas – in ourselves and in others. "A dime a dozen" is all we think they're worth.

And so the prophecy comes true. Our ideas are diminished, not because they are worthless, but because we do not know how to elicit their value. We do not understand how to cultivate them. Afraid we will be judged, or worse, fail, we discard them long before their time. Like Jack's mother of Beanstalk fame, we toss our magic beans out the window, doubting they had any real value in the first place. But they do. Jack's did. And so do yours. At least they might have value. That is, *if* you are willing to go on the journey to find out.

And that's precisely what this book is all about. Which bring us to the moment of truth. *The moment of choice.*

Ideas – no matter how exalted they might be, almost always

assume a need, desire, or intention on the part of the originator. A person must care enough about something in order to get an idea about it. The bigger one's need, desire, or intention, the greater the likelihood that ideas will make their appearance.

And so, aspiring innovator, I ask you this: What is your need, desire, or intention? What do you want to *create*? What is your idea – the "thing" you want to manifest in the world – even if seems like a long shot?

Your next step? Turn the page and describe a compelling idea or goal of yours in 25 words or less.

"If not you, who? If not now, when?"

CHOOSING

Now's the time to choose a Big Idea of *yours* that you want to manifest in the world – something you are really passionate about, even if it feels like a long shot. Maybe it's a book you want to write… or business you want to start. Maybe it's an invention you want to birth… or a career you want to change. Maybe it's something you've been wanting to do your entire life, but never had the time, support, or courage to create. Ultimately, it doesn't matter *what* it is, just as long as it's something that moves you enough to reflect on as you read this book.

Ready? Got it? Good! Now describe this idea in the space below. *And yes, it's OK to write in this book.* Not only is it OK, it's essential. Feel free to write on every page whenever a new idea, insight, or next step comes to mind. It's one of the simplest ways of breathing life into your creations-to-be…

YOUR BIG IDEA?

AUTHOR'S NOTE

Historians claim the wheel was invented in Mesopotamia, circa 3,500 BC. Until recently, I've had no reason to disbelieve their conclusion – me being a man with absolutely no access to radio carbon dating or a cousin in the archeology business. But everything changed for me on October 27, 2003. That was the day I came across an article in the New York Times detailing the discovery of some extraordinary cave paintings in the Dordogne region of France. As the article explained, Dr. Hamid Zaccharias, a Croatian archeologist, had stumbled upon one of the most remarkable discoveries of the 20th century. According to a groundbreaking study noted in the article, the cave paintings discovered by Dr. Zaccharias, along with an actual prototype, proved beyond a shadow of a doubt that the wheel was *not* invented in Mesopotamia in 3500 BC, but 24,000 years earlier by a tribe of previously unknown Neanderthals. That their invention did not impact civilization in the least was due, according to Dr. Zaccharias, to the fact that sudden seismological shifts destroyed this particular wheel-making tribe long before they could communicate their invention to the outside world.

As a committed social scientist, I found this story astounding and proceeded to devote the next four years of my life to the study of these pictographs that I might be able to understand, without any intermediaries, what was really going on for this heretofore unknown tribe of breakthrough thinkers and, more specifically, the one called "Og" – the apparent conceiver of the wheel. What follows, is my translation of the Dordogne pictographs noted here for the first time. If I have mistranslated any of the text, I ask for your understanding and forgiveness. It has been an arduous task. Please know, that in some places, I have taken liberties with the semantical and metaphorical meanings embedded in the pictographs – there being little available research on the unique symbolic language of the Neanderthals. Still, I think you will find great meaning in their story – lived so many years ago, but still so relevant today.

Mitchell Lewis Ditkoff
Woodstock, NY

The Story of Og

CHAPTER 1
OG GETS AN IDEA

Once upon a time there was a caveman named Og who had a Big Idea. It was *such* a Big Idea, in fact, that Og found it hard to sleep at night. Hard to sleep and hard to hunt and hard to do just about anything but think about his Big Idea. He thought, of course, about *telling* someone – his best friend, Ugh, perhaps, or Aargh, his devoted wife – but he just couldn't bring himself to do it, not quite sure they would actually *understand*.

Back then, when men were men and stones were stones, even the *idea* of an idea was hard to grasp. You see, for hundreds of years people had pretty much done the same thing day after day: Crouch around fires, club slow-moving animals, gorge themselves on bear meat. Most people back then didn't see the need to improve anything and those who did rarely "thought outside the cave" as Og was fond of saying.

But not Og. Og liked ideas. Og *loved* ideas. He loved them more than anything else. More than hunting. More than bear meat. More than sitting around the fire on a cold winter night and chewing the fat. Because the way Og saw it, ideas – unlike the prey he chased day after day – *came to him.* And at the oddest of times. Just before sleep. Just upon waking. Even in his dreams. In fact, it was during these times – when he least expected it – that Og began to get the first clues about his *Big Idea* – faint clues, as if a friend, many miles away, was sending him smoke signals no one else could see.

"A pile of rocks ceases to be a rock pile when somebody contemplates it with the idea of a cathedral in mind."

– St. Exupery

"To accomplish great things, we must dream as well as act."

– Anatole France

"Why is it I always get my best ideas while shaving?"

– Albert Einstein

CHAPTER 2
DAZED BY THE POSSIBILITIES

At first Og thought it was indigestion, or worse, some kind of mid-life escape from reality – a luxury no self-respecting caveman could afford, not with winter coming on. He felt dizzy. Confused. Dazed by the possibilities. It wasn't long before Og became consumed with his idea. So much so, that he soon lost interest in everything else: Hunting with his best friend, Ugh, carving bear teeth for Ogle, his son – even pounding on his hairy chest.

To the rest of the tribe, Og was *naramp poozka*. He had "rocks in his head." While they foraged and hunted, Og "what iffed" – much

"No idea is so outlandish that it should not be considered."

— Winston Churchill

to the Neanderthalic confusion of everyone else. "What if we were *all* like Og," they grumbled. "We would starve to death before the next big snow."

And so they ignored him, afraid to death that they might catch whatever it was he had.

CHAPTER 3
AARGH!

So worried was Aargh, Og's devoted wife, that she sought the council of Morf, the local medicine woman. Morf was the wisest of women and knew how to read even the most stoic caveman's face. Tuned in as she was, Morf had already heard about Og and was intrigued – especially about his curious habit of spending his days walking in circles and drawing strange little pictures on the walls of his cave.

And so she tracked Og down, fell into step behind him, and followed. Walked and watched. Watched and walked. Trailed along behind him wherever he went – saying nothing, doing nothing, just matching his movement step by step.

One week passed. Then another. And another still.

And then, with absolutely no warning one bright Neanderthalic day as they circled round and round near the mouth of Og's cave, Morf could no longer contain herself.

"Og has an *idea*!" she blurted out. "And a huge one at that. *A wooly mammoth of an idea!*"

> "Crank – a man with a new idea before it succeeds."
>
> – Mark Twain

Aargh was dumbfounded. "Idea?" she asked, combing her hair with an armadillo quill. "What mean you, 'idea'"?

Ugh nervously tapped his club on the ground. "Is it... contagious?"

> "What is now proved was once only imagined."
>
> – William Blake

Ogle winced. "Is my father going to be all right?"

But Morf just laughed. "Idea good. Idea *very* good! I no understand it yet, but Og seems... well... *better* than usual. His eyes are brighter. He's standing tall. He's making excellent use of his opposable thumb. Frankly, I haven't seen anyone this alive since Crouch.[1]

---

1 *Born 24,043 BC. Died 23,099 BC. Originator of the squatting position invented in the absence of anything to sit on.*

CHAPTER 4
THE GRUNT OF THE TOWN

*W*ord spread like the rumor of bad reindeer meat. Og, quite simply, had become the grunt of the town. But none of this mattered to him in the least. He was in another world, content to ponder, muse, imagine, and think. Content, indeed, to do nothing at all but stare at the moon.

And so it went, Og wandering in circles no one else was a part of, mumbling to himself, while the rest of the tribe went about their prehistoric business.

That is, until Ugh – Og's best friend – unable to bear the mystery any longer, tracked him down one cool night beneath a quarter moon.

7

"Where did you get it?" Ugh demanded, his brow deeply furrowed.

"Get *what?*" replied Og.

"*Idea!*" said Ugh. "Where did you get your Big Idea?"

Og shook his head. "You no understand. Me not get idea. *Idea get me.*"

Ugh just stood there. Stone-faced.

"Is true," Og went on. "Idea came to me. Like rain. Like dream. Like snake between rocks."

Ugh nodded, but didn't know why. Like the rest of the tribe, Ugh wanted to find fault with Og, but couldn't no matter how hard he tried. Maybe it was something about the look in Og's eye or the fact that the two of them had grown up in neighboring caves. Whatever it was, Ugh couldn't stop from nodding his head. Nodding and listening. Listening and nodding. And the more he did, the more Og spoke. And the more Og spoke, the more they *both* began to understand what this Big Idea was all about.

"Imagination is more important than knowledge."

– Albert Einstein

"Few people think more than two or three times a year. I've made an international reputation for myself by thinking once or twice a week."

– G.B. Shaw

After the first hour, Ugh somehow knew he didn't need to nod anymore. Just raising an eyebrow was enough to keep Og talking.

And that is how the two friends passed the night: Ugh listening, Og talking – the idea, like a gathering storm in the distance, coming more and more into focus.

"Never discourage anyone who continually makes progress, no matter how slow."

– Plato

CHAPTER 5

OG GETS AROUND TO IT

Time passed. Antelope season turned to lizard season. Lizard season turned to rabbit season. And Aargh, Og's still devoted wife, was getting angrier by the minute.

"Husband! Talk to me. Mumble! Grunt! Anything! Me have no idea what's gotten into you. *Norkle pfft.* Our relationship has hit rock bottom.

Og smiled, making Aargh's displeasure worse.

"Not time," he said. "Me not ready. And more than that, *idea* not ready."

Aargh shrugged. Aargh rolled her eyes. Aargh looked away. Aargh did all the things a woman knows how to do to make her man talk.

Og grunted, turned in her direction and spoke. "OK. I will tell you. But you must tell no one. *No one!* Do you hear?"

Og took his wife's hand and pulled her to the entrance of their cave, pointing to the full moon overhead.

"See that?" he asked.

"Yes," she replied.

"What shape it?"

"Moon shape."

"Good."

Og drew a circle in the dirt. "What *else* moon shape?"

"Sun? But…"

"Wait. Og not done. When tribe meets beneath full moon, how we sit?"

"We… sit… around the fire."

"Exactly," gushed Og. "We are moon shape. Sun shape."

Aargh was lost.

"I invent nothing. I rediscover."

– August Rodin

"I'll play it first and tell you what it is later."

– Miles Davis

"You see, dear wife. There is something about *round*. It is everywhere we look."

"Me…. no understand," answered Aargh.

"You will," sighed Og. "You will."

"Whenever anything is being accomplished, it is being done, I have learned, by a monomaniac with a mission."

– Peter Drucker

CHAPTER 6

OG'S HEAD IS FULL, BUT THE CUPBOARD IS EMPTY

*I*t had been two months since Og hunted with the tribe – two months of pondering what Morf had called his "Big Idea." Two months of staring at sagebrush and the moon and seeing new connections between the two even he did not understand. Only the kindness of Ugh had kept meat on the table. But meat was not enough and Aargh was at her wit's end, egged on daily by her mother, Nudge, who had come to share their cave for the long, cold winter.

"*Morga hinem laku,*" groaned Aargh. "I cannot take it anymore. Everywhere I go, people grunt behind your back. Our cupboard is empty. Something must change – and soon!"

Og stroked his beard.

"Worry not, woman. I have gone to Honch[2] and asked for time to speak idea at next Big Meating. Surely, this will make big difference.

Aargh turned the color of week-old antelope meat.

"Have you lost what's left of your mind, husband? You know what happens at those meatings! Remember how they treated Rrow, the one with the so-called arrowhead idea?"

"Oh...yes.... I do," chuckled Og, letting out a long slow whistle. "They never got the point, did they?"

"Never got the point?" Aargh shrieked. "They wouldn't let him complete a single sentence. He died a broken caveman."

"This be different," Og replied. "My idea better than arrowhead. Much better."

> "*There is a vitality, a life force, an energy, that is translated to you into action, and because there is only one of you in all time, this expression is unique. If you block it, it will never exist through any other medium and will be lost.*"
>
> – Martha Graham

> "*The act of creation is first of all an act of destruction.*"
>
> – Pablo Picasso

---

2 *The Boss, The Big Kahuna, CEO (Chief Evolution Officer).*

CHAPTER 7
THE BIG MEATING

The next few days flew by quickly, Og doing his best to round out his idea, Aargh doing her best to round up new things for her mother to eat. And all the while the village was awash in rumors. Some said Og was crazy. Some said he was possessed. Others said he'd stolen something more precious than fire from the Gods. But Honch paid no attention, focused only on getting ready for the Big Meating – the time, beneath the next full moon, when the tribe would gather around the fire to *bozong lamu* – chew the fat.

The Meating began, as it had for years, with the ritual eating of bison feet and Honch raising his oversized "talking club" in his powerful right hand.

"Good people," he began, "we meat tonight at Og's request. He has, claims Morf, a Big Idea."

No one spoke.

"Before Idea Man begins," continued Honch, "let me remind you of the Meating Rules – handed down for centuries by our revered ancestors – just in case you feel the need to speak."

RULE #1: Chew first, listen later.

RULE #2: If you listen, do not listen long.

RULE #3: Make no eye contact.

RULE #4: Interrupt every chance you get.

RULE #5: Use humor like a weapon.

"Any questions? No? Good. Let's begin. Og?"

Og stood to his full height and walked slowly around the circle. All eyes were not upon him.

"What I speak about tonight, dear friends, is not *my* idea. But neither did I steal it. It was given to me."

Blitz poked Oomph in the ribs.

Mook picked fleas from his beard.

Nuk passed more than judgment.

"Some people have a way with words – others not have way."

– Steve Martin

"The new idea either finds a champion or it dies. No ordinary involvement with a new idea provides the energy required to cope with the indifference and resistance that change provokes.

– Tom Peters

"I can tell by the look in your eyes that you have questions, but first I have one for you: How do you get from your cave to the forest when it's time to hunt?'"

"Walk! "shouted Blitz. "We walk."

"Yes," replied Og. "And how do you get dead meat from forest *back* to caves?"

"More walk!" shouted Blitz again. "Walk and *drag*."

"Yes, again, my stoop-shouldered friend. And that is quite a drag, isn't it – trying to get all that meat such long distance? *Well... I have found a better way.*"

Total silence.

Tribal silence.

The silence of people with small vocabularies and large foreheads.

"Better way?" bellowed Honch. "*Better way?* Not possible. We be walking and dragging for years."

Zook jumped to his feet, his face suddenly red. "It took Zook ten years to perfect dragging technique. Dragging good. Dragging very good."

"In the beginner's mind there are many possibilities, in the expert's mind, there are few."

– Shunryu Suzuki

"Not everything that counts can be counted; and not everything that can be counted counts."

– Albert Einstein

Nimbo pulled Zook's hair. Honch yawned.

But Og kept on.

Reaching into his bearskin wrap, he pulled out a piece of tree bark with what seemed to be some kind of odd markings. Unfolding it once, twice, three times, he held it high overhead.

"Fellow hunters and gatherers, sons and daughters of Zilch.[3] I introduce to you a way to improve all our lives and future of world – the *wheel!*"

Nobody spoke.

Nobody spoke again.

"Looks like picture of stone sun to me," laughed Zoup.

"Hrumph," hrumphed Hrumph. "Three months wait for *this*? A picture of a… *round thing?*"

But Og continued. "It *not* sun. It *not* moon. It is *wheel* – round thing that rolls… a thing that moves along ground capable of carrying load with least amount of effort."

Honch laughed. Oomph laughed. Soon *everyone* was laughing.

"Man is so constituted as to see what is wrong with a new thing, not what is right. To verify this, you have but to submit a new idea to a committee."

– Charles Kettering

---

3 The Neanderthalic *God of Hunting*.

"Wheel no good," barked Negoh. "It will roll away. Then gone."

"Wheel bad," barked Nuk. "Enemies take it. Then *they* will have it and *we* won't."

"Wheel worse than bad," added Bork. "We have no roads. What will wheel roll on?"

On and on it went. The darts. The arrows. The eyebrows raised like spears. Og shot a quick glance at Aargh. Then at Ugh. Then looked to the full moon overhead and bit his lip, a single tear in his left eye rolling slowly down his cheek.

"A new idea is delicate. It can be killed by a sneer or a yawn. It can be stabbed to death by a quip, and worried to death by a frown on the right man's brow."

– Charlie Brower

CHAPTER 8

THE PATH IS MADE
BY WALKING ON IT

O g felt bad. Very bad. Bad as a caveman can feel. Dense like the age he lived in. Thick like his matted beard.

The worse he felt, the more he wanted to run. Get away. Disappear. Leave the tribe once and for all.

Aargh was the first to notice Og was having a hard time, but had no idea what to do. If she approached her husband, he would only retreat further into their cave. If she ignored him, he would feel abandoned – and she would lose him once again to the deepest caverns of his own disappointment.

It was into this world of prehistoric bewilderment that Ogle, Og's only son, appeared.

"Big Daddy," he said. "What wrong?"

Og could barely hear the boy, consumed as he was by endless images of spinning and rolling.

Og looked at Ogle, then to his feet, then to the hundreds of pictures he had drawn on the walls.

But he didn't look long, his looking now interrupted by a sound at the entrance of the cave. It was Ugh, breathing much faster than normal. "Og! Big news. Me have big news. It is Crouch! He has sent for you!"

"Crouch?" Og repeated, turning around. *"Crouch?"*

"Yes. *Him*," said Ugh, "Crouch has heard of your idea. Wants to see you. Now!"

"But.... Crouch lives far away, high in mountains, many days from here."

Ugh moved in quick circles, trying to think of something to say.

"There is only one thing stronger than all the armies in the world and that is an idea whose time has come."

– Victor Hugo

"Conclusions arrived at through reasoning have very little or no influence in altering the course of our lives."

– Carlos Casteneda

"Crouch knows, my friend. *He knows!*"

"Not possible," said Og. "And not only that, there's no way there! No way. No road. No path."

Ugh opened his mouth to reply, but it was Ogle who spoke.

"Big Daddy, do not worry. Crouch is closer than you think. And besides, isn't the path made by walking on it?"

"Do not be afraid to take a big step when one is indicated. You can't cross a chasm in two small jumps."

– David Lloyd George

CHAPTER 9
CROUCH

*I*t took Og 30 days to get to Crouch's abode, one complete cycle of the moon. But to him it seemed only like the blink of an eye, consumed as he was by the going. Before he knew it, there he was, high on the mountain, staring at Crouch squatting in the position now bearing his name.

"*Glanu fligby nanoo,*[4]" proclaimed Crouch. "Welcome! Idea Man. I've been expecting you."

"You have?" asked Og, crouching low in reverence.

Crouch smiled. "Stand up, friend. The so-called crouch is highly overrated. Speak!"

---

4 Yo!

Og stood.

"But… Crouch, *you* are the one who should be speaking! *You* were the one who changed the way we stood our ground."

Crouch sighed. "I am not going to tell you my story, Og. I have told it too often. What is true for me may not be true for you. The only way to know what I have learned is to live your *own* story – not listen to me talk about the past so it seems I've understood something worthy of the telling."

Og frowned.

"What I *will* tell you, Idea Man, is the story *behind* my story. That is, *if* you want to get the Big Idea out of your head and into the world. And even more importantly, *if* you want to understand how to enjoy the journey."

Og found the nearest log, sat down, opened his eyes wider and listened.

"You can expect no influence if you are not susceptible to influence."

– Carl Jung

"New organs of perception come into being as a result of necessity. Therefore, increase your necessity, so that you may increase your perception."

– Rumi

CHAPTER 10

AN ARROW TO THE HEART OF THE MATTER

"Once upon a time," began Crouch, "there was a man named Namoo, a most gifted archer. Time and again, Namoo would enter archery tournaments and win. He won so often and so convincingly that word of his accomplishments soon spread. By the time he was 19, Namoo was known throughout the land.

One day, upon returning home from yet another victory, Namoo found himself rushing through a marketplace and bumping into an old man carrying a basket of potatoes. Potatoes went flying everywhere and the old man fell to the ground with a thud."

"Old man!" shouted Namoo, "Get out of my way! Don't you know who I am?"

The old man looked up, squinting.

"Oh yes, I know who you are," he replied. "You are Namoo. Second best archer in all the land."

"*Second* best?" shouted Namoo. "*Second*? I am … *best*. No one can beat me."

The old man smiled as he stood, slowly gathering his potatoes. "Yes, you are great! But there is one even greater than you!"

"Greater than me? Impossible! Who is this imposter? Where does he live?"

"Oh," the old man said slowly, as if entering a temple. "His name is Master Po. He lives many miles to the North – high atop Mt. Kalum."

"Then I will challenge him," Namoo bellowed, "and put an end to such nonsense!"

Pushing his way past the old man, the young archer stormed off. For two moons he walked. Through underbrush and overgrowth. Through overbrush and undergrowth.

"If you lose the power to laugh, you lose the power to think."

– Clarence Darrow

"You can only be as good as you dare to be bad."

– John Barrymore

When he finally arrived at the foot of Mt. Kalum, Namoo could not believe his eyes. The mountain was sheer rock face, covered with ice and pitched at a 90 degree angle straight to the top, hidden by clouds. A lesser man would have ended his journey there. But not Namoo. He climbed.

On the 8th day of his ascent, the young archer somehow found himself at the top and seeing what appeared to be a little old man sitting on a blanket.

"Welcome wayfarer, I have been expecting you."

The young archer took the deepest of breaths. "I… am… Namoo, best archer in all the land. I… I challenge you!"

The old man smiled, bowed once, then looked to the sky.

"Very well, as you are my guest, please go first."

Without hesitation, Namoo grabbed an arrow from his quiver, notched it on the string of his immense bow, closed an eye, tilted his head, looked up, drew the string back, and with all of his might let the arrow fly. As it neared the

"You can't solve a problem at the same level it was created. You have to rise above it to the next level."

– Albert Einstein

"We don't know a millionth of one percent about anything."

– Thomas Edison

top of its flight, he pulled a second from the quiver and shot it high, halving the first in two and, in a rapid succession of ten, continued, each arrow splitting the one before it, arrow halves landing in a perfect circle around the seated master and making the ancient sound of "Hmm" upon entering the ground.

"Hmm," said Master Po. "Impressive. Most impressive. Now, I believe, it is *my* turn."

Reaching behind him where there *would* have been a quiver if he *had* a quiver, he pulled what *would* have been an arrow if he had an arrow, notched what *would* have been a string on what *would* have been a bow, closed one eye, pulled slowly, paused for what seemed like eternity, and then – in slow motion pantomime – let go.

Smiling ever so slightly, he turned to the puzzled challenger.

"*You*, my friend" said Master Po, "have mastered the art of shooting with a bow and arrow. *I,* on the other hand, have mastered the art of shooting *without* a bow and arrow. Know this: *It is not just* what *you do. It is* how *you do it.*"

"When an archer misses his mark, he turns and looks to the fault within himself. Failure to hit the bulls-eye is never the fault of the target. To improve your aim – improve yourself."

– Gilbert Arland

"Now that we have met with paradox, we have some hope of making progress."

– Niels Bohr

CHAPTER 11
NOTHING TO GET

O g just sat there. Stunned.[5]

"I.... I.... I... don't get it."

Crouch sprang to his feet.

"That's the point, Idea Man! *There's nothing to get!* Nothing to get and nothing to do. Nothing to do and nowhere to go. Nowhere to go and no way to get there. All trying is useless. The effort we need to make is the effort of no effort."

Og rocked back and forth.

"Listen, Og. There are two worlds. One is the world you see. The other is the world you do not see. The world you see is the world of

---

5 "Stunned" from the *Latin, "stoynum," meaning "silent like a stone."*

"this and that" – the world of reindeer meat and wooly mammoths, fire and ice, wives and husbands. It is the world in which the thing you call 'idea' comes true… or not."

"The *other* world, the world of Master Po, is the cave of the heart, the source – a world that does not need to be proved or *improved*. No disillusionment is there because there is no illusion. No disenchantment is there because there is no enchantment. No disappointment is there because there are no appointments. It is what exists *before* you think up ideas to make things better. It is from *this* world that the idea for the wheel first came to be."

Og slapped his forehead. "But isn't this what separates us from the animals we hunt – to think big thoughts?"

Crouch crouched low. "Og, why do you think your idea for the wheel has not come to pass yet? It is not because the wheel is not a 'good' idea. It is! It is even *better* than the crouch."

"Because it is an idea before its time?" Og shrugged.

"No."

"Obstacles are those frightful things you see when you take your eyes off the goal."
– Hannah Moore

"In order to do something, one has to be something."
– Goethe

"Because the tribe is stuck in the past?"

"No."

"Because people are afraid of change?"

"No. No. No. The reason your idea has not come into being is because *you* have not come into being. That and the fact that you have been trying too hard. Unlike, the wheel (or the sagebrush you've been seeing everywhere) you are not *rolling*. You are not revolving around the hub of your inspiration. You are *dragging* your idea behind you like a dead animal. And when you are not doing that, you are *pushing* it. Neither works."

Crouch took a deep breath. "My dear Og, you have a lot to learn. But do not worry. You will learn it, though not from me. The *idea* will be your teacher. And the tribe."

"But… I came all this way. And *you* have already been where I am going. Won't you tell me *something*?"

Crouch threw his head back, laughed, then drew three circles in the dirt with a crooked finger.

"If you insist, my friend."

"The less effort, the faster and more powerful you will be."

– Bruce Lee

"There's not much difference between being a genius and not having a clue."

– Roone Arledge

CIRCLE #1: *Be the idea.* Don't just have the idea.

CIRCLE #2: *Show them.* People need to see what seizes you.

CIRCLE #3: *Include the tribe.* Circles can include or exclude. Choose inclusion.

And with that, Crouch picked up the long log he was sitting on and rolled it down the mountain.

"Have faith, Og! Just like idea came to you, so will the way to express it. Above all, do not worry. Worry will bleed you of the idea. Know that you are caretaker of something grand. In fact, I have the feeling that one day you will be spokesman for *more* than just wheel, but the place from where *all* ideas come."

"Place? What place?" asked Og.

But Crouch simply laughed, stood, and walked away.

"A little girl told me she liked radio more than television because the pictures were so much more beautiful."

— Joseph Chilton Pearce

"Adversity reveals genius. Prosperity obscures it."

— Horatio

CHAPTER 12

SMOKE FROM A FIRE, FLAKES FROM A STONE

O g just stood there. He had no idea what to do. His mind, like a small burrowing animal, frantically looked for a place to hide. Thoughts, like vultures, filled his head, circling as he took his first unsure steps down the steep mountain away from Crouch.

How he got down Og had no idea, but there he was in the valley and seeing, off in the distance, the vague outlines of his remembered village.

He could see smoke from a fire. He could hear voices echoing off stone. But even louder he could hear the words of Crouch echoing inside him: *"Be the idea... show them... include the tribe."*

Og understood. He must not return empty-handed. The long neglected hunter inside him had to feed the tribe's hunger for proof. *And soon.*

"Ideas won't keep. Something must be done about them."

– A.N. Whitehead

He reached inside the otter skin bag he wore around his neck and retrieved the small hand-axe so long unused. Like a flag into battle, he held it high overhead. And then, just steps away, he saw it, the unmoving prey at the end of his hunt – the perfect boulder. About the height of his son. Almost round from what must have been a long rolling downwards.

"By your stumbling the world is perfected."

– Sri Aurobindo

Og's breathing slowed and then his thoughts, approaching as he might a bear at the end of a long hibernation. Eyes wide, head bowed, he brought the axe-blade down. But not to kill. No. This was a much finer motion, more like the stripping of bark from a branch he would use for a walking stick.

Stroke by stroke he chiseled and cut, faster and faster, chipping, rounding the edges, finding the curves of the full moon in it.

Hours passed. Days.

And then, just before he was done, flakes of stone at his feet like ashes from a long night's ceremonial fire, Og remembered the *tribe*. Bowing once in the direction of Zilch, he chiseled their names into the center of the wheel: Aargh, his devoted wife, Ogle, his only son, Ugh, his best friend, Honch, Morf, Nudge, Nuk. And above all, Crouch, living so many miles away, high in the mountains. Alone.

"With love, even the rocks will open."

– Hazrat Inayat Khan

"The mark of an artist is how much he throws away."

– Johannes Brahms

CHAPTER 13

THE HAPPY ACCIDENT

O g was tired. Very tired. He would have slept for days if it was darker, but the first rays of morning light were upon him and he knew it was time to go. Crouching low, he reached as far as he could around the wheel, grunted, and pulled with his full might. The wheel stood.

All day he moved, shepherd to this herd of one. Over bones he traveled. Over branches, stones, and moss, doing his best to stay on the path made clear from the many feet of those who had gone before him. And when the wheel fell, as it did more times than he could count, Og simply bent to retrieve it – his bending more a bowing to a God he couldn't see than a man on a mission.

That he could move at all is a mystery even to this day. Something was pushing Og as hard as he was pushing the wheel. And whatever *it* was never got tired. A puma ran by. A water buffalo. Three men from a neighboring tribe. But no one attacked, amazed at the sight of this strange man grunting, heaving, pushing a... *something* up a hill.

At the top, catching what was left of his breath, Og stopped to wipe his brow. And as he did, the wheel began to turn on its own. Away from him. Down the hill. Faster and faster.

Og chased after it.

And then...

WHACK!!!

A sound like thunder.

A sound like trouble.

A sound like the end of the world.

The wheel had crashed very far away from Og and come to a full stop.

When Og, out of breath, finally arrived, he could not believe his eyes. *The center was gone!* Where once was stone, now was.... nothing.

"Beginnings are always messy."

– John Galsworthy

"You will never find the time for anything. If you want time, you must make it."

– Charles Burton

The crash had shattered the center of the wheel exactly along the lines where Og had chiseled the names of the tribe. The center was missing. The center was gone. The center was empty. But not as empty as Og. All this work! ALL THIS WORK! *And for what?*

Og sat down and cried.

"Security is mostly a superstition. Life is either a daring adventure or nothing."

– Helen Keller

CHAPTER 14

THE CENTER IS EVERYTHING

*H*ow much time passed like this, Og could not tell. All he knew was he had nothing to show for his efforts – only this round thing with a gaping hole in the middle. Confused, he extended an arm to touch what was left of his creation, fully expecting it to break into a thousand pieces. But it did not. It just lay there. Like the sun, like the moon, only *lighter* now that its center was gone. Og stood and pulled the wheel to its full height. Somehow, the wheel was easier to *balance* than before. Easier to *push*. There was even a place *inside*

it for Og to sit and ride when he was too tired to walk.

And so he moved. Step by step. Turn by turn. Closer and closer to home. As the wheel turned, so did his thoughts, now focused on the *center* of the wheel and how it might *connect* to something else.

The faster he thought, the faster he walked. The faster he walked, the faster the wheel turned. The faster the wheel turned, the faster he thought. Until he could think no more.

That's when Og looked up.

The full moon was shining.

"Genius is infinite painstaking."

— Michelangelo

"I am looking for a lot of people who have an infinite capacity to not know what can't be done."

— Henry Ford

CHAPTER 15

OG SLEPT LIKE
A ROCK

Og reached his village just before dawn, glad no one was awake to question his arrival. Exhausted, he simply leaned the wheel against the entrance to his cave, walked in, and fell into a heap next to his sleeping wife and child.

He slept like a rock.

Og may have slept like a rock, but he snored like a bear – and loud enough to wake his son still dreaming of his father's long delayed return. Ogle, living up to his name, *ogled* – uncontrollably staring at the man almost everyone else in the tribe was sure had gone insane. Or worse, had gone *away*, leaving his family to follow nothing but a Big Idea. How long Ogle ogled no one knows for sure. But what we do know is this: Og's snoring soon turned to grunts and his grunts soon turned to words – barely understandable moanings from what seemed like another world. The more Og spoke,[6] the faster his son's mind raced – and the more it raced, the closer he found himself to the entrance of the cave where the *round thing* was. Grunting, he tried to push, but the round thing would not move.

"Confusion is a word we've invented for an order that is not yet understood."

– Henry Miller

"What's this all about?" Ogle muttered to himself. *"How does the round thing work?"*

Confused, he looked to Aargh, snoring lightly next to Og. And then it dawned. Not the day, but a thought. A good thought. A big thought. Maybe even a Big Idea thought. His mother had carried him before he could walk. The wheel would have to carry, too. *What if…"*

---

6 Og didn't speak. He *spoke*. How could he not, consumed as he was with everything wheel-like?

Ogle sprang to his feet, kissed his sleeping mother on the cheek, his sleeping father on the brow and ran, like a boy being chased by a very large reptile, out of the cave.

"The greatest invention in the world is the mind of a child."

– Thomas Edison

CHAPTER 16
FOLLOW YOUR FEET

O gle had no clue where to go, but he didn't need to. His feet did. And when he got there – to the cave of Nema, daughter of Ugh, he knew exactly what to do: *wake her…* wake her and ask her to do the unthinkable – borrow her father's tools for some late night *poofta.*[7]

Ogle touched her lightly on the shoulder. Nema woke and knew, in a flash, it was time to go. Not because Ogle woke her. No. And not because he asked for her father's tools. No again. *Because of the look in his eyes.* And so she stood, said nothing, took his hand and, step by step with the son of the man with the Big Idea, quickly left the cave.

---

7 No. It's not what you think. "Poofta" is caveman slang for "experiment."

"Without a deadline, baby, I wouldn't do nothing."

– Duke Ellington

"The lightning spark of thought generated in the solitary mind awakens its likeness in another."

– Thomas Carlyle

"Intuition will tell the thinking mind where to look next."

– Dr. Jonas Salk

As the two of them ran to the forest, Ogle told her of his father's return, the round thing at the entrance of the cave, the way it looked, the way it felt, the hole in the center, and the strange words his father spoke from sleep. The more he talked, the more she nodded. The more she nodded, the more he spoke – both feeling themselves lighter than ever… circling the moment like some kind of prehistoric bird riding unseen currents of air as it descended down upon its prey.

Something had a hold of them – something they could not see. It moved their feet, their eyes, the way they stood. It knew exactly what to look for on the ground, what materials to choose, and what to do with tools no longer heavy in their hands. And as they moved from here to there and back again, they sang: *"Two hands, two feet, two eyes, two ears. It takes two for something moomba[8] to appear."*

And so it went for the rest of the night, Ogle and Nema singing, Ogle and Nema laughing – trying this, trying that, and when nothing else worked, trying the other thing, too.

---

8 Amazing, beautiful, sacred, holy, and practical

CHAPTER 17
EVERYONE'S TURN

When Og woke in the morning he had no idea where he was. Zero. Zippo. Zilch. At least not until he saw Aargh, his devoted wife, standing at the entrance of their cave, hands on her hips, staring at the wheel. But not just Aargh was staring. No. Grunt had gotten out in the middle of the night. Ugh was there, too. And Morf. And Nuk. And Honch. And Oomph. And every other member of the now chattering tribe.

They stooped. They gaped. They scratched.

"Look," laughed Nuk, "a giant donut[9]."

"No way!" said Hrrumph. "It's a stone bead for the Gods."

---

9 Nuk was the first known clairvoyant. Some say he always had a glazed look in his eye.

"Fat chance," barked Nook. "It's a petrified bagel.[10]

Og remained silent, familiar as he was with this ancient tribal ritual. Lost in his silence, he did not notice the heads turning away. Something had caught their attention. And that something was a sound. *The sound of rolling. The sound of a round thing. The sound of a wheel creaking and turning over sticks and stones.* But not just a wheel – a wheel *connected* to something. And not just a something for something's sake, but a something with a purpose. Behind this wheel, attached by a few newly carved lengths of wood and some craftily tied saplings, was some kind of container – a hollowed out piece of wood big enough for a healthy chunk of bear meat. The contraption[11] was not rolling by itself. It was being pushed, Ogle on one handle, Nema on the other – both of them being followed by the rest of the children in the tribe.

"Whoa!" exclaimed Nuk.

"If you do not express your own original ideas, if you do not listen to your own being, you will have betrayed yourself. Also you will have betrayed your community in failing to make your contribution to the whole."

– Rollo May

---

10 Nook, the first Jewish caveman, got most of his good ideas from Nuk.

11 The first known wheelbarrow.

"Double whoa!" exclaimed Oomph.

"Double whoa and a large armadillo," exclaimed Nook.

A great volcano of words rumbled inside the tribe.

Aargh was the first to speak. She had the look of fire in her eyes.

"Og... ooh... ah... now I *see*! But more than that, I think I have what you once had — a *Big Idea*. It's been growing in me since you left the cave — something for the children. A flat piece of wood with wheels on bottom. I call it "*skabrd.*[12]" See? I have one here I made last week with my own hands."

Ugh now stood. "Og, I also have a *Big Idea*. It's bowls and pots we make with wheels we turn with busy feet.[13] Look! I have a small drawing here."

Oomph, rising from the biggest bump on the biggest log, stood to his full height. "*Schmorka moodle vurpa!*[14] I've had my idea

"The greater the contrast, the greater the potential. Great energy only comes from a correspondingly great tension of opposites.

– Carl Jung

---

12 The first known skateboard.
13 The first known pottery wheel.
14 Why are you reading this arcane footnote? Shouldn't you be doing something meaningful to move ahead with *your* Big Idea? Yes, I know there's more to this book, but *now's* the time to take your next step. You can read the rest later tonight...

since I was small, but no one to tell. It's way to carry fire through rain. Fire not get wet. *Umbrelloo* is the name."

On and on it went. All day long. All night, too – one cave dweller after the next doing their best to find the words to talk about their ideas. Big ideas. Small ideas. Round ideas. Square ideas. New ideas. Old ideas. And all to help their tribe... and the *next* tribe... and the bears... and the birds... and the armadillos.

And then, just when the last person had taken their turn, a small man approached from the very last row, walking in a way no one had ever seen before. Slowly, like he had no place special to go. But quickly, too, like he couldn't quite wait to get there. Og recognized him immediately. It was Crouch, laughing softly, saying nothing, only pointing to the full moon overhead...

"Neither a lofty degree of intelligence, nor imagination, nor both together, go to making genius. Love, love, love. That is the soul of genius."

– Mozart

POSTSCRIPT:

Regrettably, dear reader, this is where the story ends. What happened next may never be known. According to Dr. Hamid Zaccharias, the last set of pictographs drawn on the back walls of Og's cave no longer exist — due, he believes, to seismological shifts or a long series of invasions by neighboring tribes during the tumultuous years that followed. Fortunately, one additional piece of Og's story has recently been discovered in a small cave just three miles from his original dwelling. Apparently, in the last days before his death, Og was asked by Honch to record his "key learnings" for future members of the tribe. What follows are 12 of those 13 (what we might call "best practices") translated into modern English for easy understanding. The 13th and final one, according to Dr. Zaccharias, has either been destroyed or is yet to be discovered.

"*I start where the last man left off.*"

– Thomas Edison

What Og Learned

12 WHEELY GOOD BEST PRACTICES

1. You don't get an idea – an idea gets you

2. Get comfortable with discomfort

3. Think outside the cave

4. Ask dumb questions

5. Immerse

6. Find someone who will really listen to you

7. Eat feedback, digest what you can

8. Prototype

9. If you want a breakthrough, take a break

10. Play with your idea

11. Have an intention

12. Make new connections

1. YOU DON'T GET AN IDEA —

AN IDEA GETS YOU

People ask Og where he got his Big Idea. This is the wrong question. *Og did not get the idea. The idea got Og.* Got him like fire gets wood. Like trees get wind. Og wasn't the creator, only the *receiver.* He was the entrance to a cave and the idea walked in. The idea made its home in him. And stayed. Og knows his tribe thinks he invented the wheel. But this is not true. *The wheel invented Og.* It changed the way he walked. It changed the way he thought. It changed the way he slept and woke and looked at things. *Here's what Og says:* Get out of the way! Be willing to receive the Big Idea. Og's effort was not heroic. It was only the effort to be seized. Don't waste your time thinking you are so smart. You don't get the Big Idea. The Big Idea gets you.

"I am a fool, oh yes, I am confused. Other men are clear and bright. But I alone am dim and weak. Other men are sharp and clever. But I alone am dull and stupid. Oh, I drift like the waves of the sea, without direction, like the restless wind."

— Lao Tzu

2. GET COMFORTABLE

WITH DISCOMFORT

Just before Og got his Big Idea, he felt really bad. Like he had just eaten a really large armadillo. No matter what he did, he couldn't get comfortable. His skin felt too small. He couldn't stand still, but neither did he want to sit. The tribe thought something was wrong. They asked if Og was sick, but Og was not sick – only sick of being stuck between a rock and hard place. Only now does Og see that discomfort was good. *It moved him.* It freed him from his past. Like a rock slide, it loosened things up. Discomfort became his guide. Even when Og stumbled it was good. At least he stumbled forward. *Og says this:* If you want to birth a Big Idea, make friends with discomfort. Sometimes feeling bad is just a clue that something good is on its way.

"The statue is already in the stone, had been in the stone since the beginning of time. The sculptor's job is to see it and release it by carefully scraping away the excess material."

– Michelangelo

3. THINK OUTSIDE THE CAVE

Og loves his cave. It protects him from rain and bears and the feeling that the world is too big. But sometimes Og's cave feels too small. It's protection *confines* – especially when he wants to think something new. That's when its walls are too close. Makes him see the same things every day. Same shadows. Same rocks. Same thoughts about same shadows and rocks. That's when his cave becomes a *cage.* That's when Og needs to leave his cave like a snake its skin. Only then can Og see new things and, more than that, *new connections between things.* That's the time Og can see that moon and rolling sagebrush are related. That's when he sees things he cannot see in his cave – the cave of no sagebrush… the cave of no wind… the cave of no distances. *Og says this:* If you want a Big Idea, see beyond the walls of what you know. Think outside the cave.

"The silly question is the first intimation of some totally new development."

– A.N. Whitehead

4. ASK DUMB QUESTIONS

There is one thing good about being a Neanderthal. *We don't know much.* And what we *do* know, we don't think about much. This is good. This is very good. It frees us from the past. It frees us to ask questions others call "dumb" – questions children might ask. It's good to be dumb. Dumb gives you new eyes. Dumb takes you beyond your ancestor's beliefs of what's possible. So *be* dumb. But don't be stupid. There is a big difference.

Being dumb is not knowing. Being stupid is forgetting what you already know to be true. Og chooses to be dumb. That's why he's smart. *Og says this:* Don't take "know" for an answer. Ask dumb questions. It's when you *think* you know, that Big Ideas keep their distance.

5. IMMERSE!

When cavemen hunt, they go on a long journey and don't return for days. The further they get from home, the more they hear, the more they see, the more they catch the scent of moose or antelope many miles away. Senses become sharp like the animals they seek. They see shapes in the darkness they could not see by day. *Magno fluma weh.* They become immersed – saturated with purpose. This immersion is less a state of mind, than it is a state of mindlessness – the place all people visit in sleep. Immersed, we are sponges, soaking up what we need with our belly, not our brain. In this place, we are free of distraction, free of doubt, free of the tasks of survival. *Og knows this:* Immersion is the key to the land of Big

"Change your thoughts and you change the world."

– N. Vincent Peale

Ideas. It is the father of perseverance. It is the mother of discovery. It is the umbilical cord to whatever needs to be born.

6. Find someone who will really listen to you

An idea unspoken is like a fire unstarted. It exists, but only in your mind. Its heat warms no one but you. Its light illumines nothing. Sometimes, I know, an idea needs to *stay* unspoken – not because it is bad, but because it is not yet ready to be heard. Speak an idea too soon and you will ruin it – fruit picked before its time. Wait too long and it will rot. *Hear Og now:* If you want your Big Idea to come alive find someone who will really listen to you – someone who really cares about you *and* your idea like a mother her child. Their attention alone will be enough to fan the flames of your imagining. But be careful! Choose no one whose listening is merely a pause before speech. Then what seems to be their attention will only be a cage for your idea.

"I refuse to be intimidated by reality anymore. What is reality? Nothing but a collective hunch."

– Lily Tomlin

7. EAT FEEDBACK, DIGEST WHAT YOU CAN

There are three things cavemen hate: Being attacked by someone with a bigger spear, being eaten by a reptile, and being told what they think is wrong. All three have the same thing in common – *territory* – and the invasion of it. It is in this place where cavemen are most vulnerable. Is there anyone you know who likes their territory being invaded? No one does! Not even Crouch. And because we don't, we guard ourselves. Withdraw. Retract. *Withhold* ideas from others with all our might. *Og says this:* Eat feedback, chew on it, digest what you can. Even if it tastes bitter, nourishment is there. Sometimes what others say will be useful. Sometimes not. In either case, you will be served. And more than that, your idea will be served. Feedback is not the enemy. Your fear of feedback is the enemy.

"Sometimes, when I find I haven't written a single sentence after scribbling whole pages, I collapse on my couch and lie there dazed, bogged in a swamp of despair, hating and blaming myself…A quarter of an hour later, everything has changed, my heart is pounding with joy."

– Gustave Flaubert

8. PROTOTYPE

Og knows he made some big mistakes along the way – especially in the beginning. Here's one: Og brought a *picture* of the wheel to the Big Meating, not the wheel itself. Tribe was hungry to know, but all Og brought was a *menu*. Og gave people food for thought, but nothing for their bellies. Yes, a picture is better than nothing at all. It may even be *morzo* – worth a thousand words. But a thousand words is worth nothing to the deaf. And without proof from Og, the tribe did not hear a single word he said. *Og says this:* If you want others to know about your Big Idea, get real. Show them. Make a prototype that works.

"There is always an element of chance and you must be willing to live with that element. If you insist on certainty, you will paralyze yourself."

– J.P. Getty

9. IF YOU WANT A BREAKTHROUGH, TAKE A BREAK

There is a thought Neanderthals have that is dumber than a stone: *The more you try, the better your result.* Logical? Yes. True? No. Trying doesn't always work. Sometimes, only *not* trying works. You can't make a tree grow faster by pulling on it's leaves. *Og says this:* If you want a breakthrough, take a break. Leave what you're doing and do something else. When you take the time to do something different, something different will take the time to happen to you. Clean your spear. Make a fire. Pick some berries. *Anything* to take your mind off your Big Idea.

10. PLAY WITH YOUR IDEA

Ideas are like small children. They need a lot of love and attention. If you want your ideas to have a good life, get down to their level. Hold them close to you. Play their games, especially when you think you have something *else* to do. Then they will thrive. Then they will grow. Then they will let you in on their little secrets. *Og says this:* It takes a lot of work to help your ideas grow up, but more than that, it takes a lot of *play*. Have some fun with your idea! Be willing to see it through the eyes of a child.

"The creation of something new is not accomplished by the intellect, but by the play instinct arising from inner necessity. The creative mind plays with the object it loves."

– Carl Jung

11. HAVE AN INTENTION

Most Neanderthals have the same basic things: Cave, club, big chin, and the instinct to survive. Og has no problem with this. We are who we are. But if our tribe hopes to survive, we need one more thing: *Intention*. What does

Og mean by this? Focused impulse. Sacred wish. Sustained thought that does not need to be thought about, only savored. Og had this with the wheel. It was more than a need. More than a want. More than desire. It kept him going when nothing else did. *Og says this:* Idea is the seed of all possibility. *Intention* is the wind that carries the seed into the world.

"Sit, walk, or run, but don't wobble."

– Zen proverb

"When you ask creative people how they did something, they feel a little guilty because they didn't really do it, they just saw something. It seemed obvious to them after a while. That's because they were able to connect experiences they've had and synthesize new things."

–Steve Jobs

12. Make new connections

When cavemen return from the hunt their children want to know *where* we found our prey. And *how*. For the young ones, the story of the hunt is more nourishment than the meat we bring. Like the ground we sleep on, their question is hard to answer. *Og says this*: Big Idea is like a big puzzle. The pieces must be put together. But some pieces don't fit until you find new pieces, *not* in the puzzle, to connect them to. During his journey Og saw many connections – especially the connection between how the tribe sits *around* fire, the rolling sagebrush, and the moon. This turned Og's head around. And this turning head soon led him to the turning wheel.

Tooling Up

TOOLING UP

35 Ways to Get the Wheels Turning

As Og's earthly representative, I have been designing and leading creative thinking sessions for a wide range of corporations since 1986. I have worked with left-brained people, right-brained people, and air-brained people – all of whom have been interested in "getting out of the box." In the process of providing my service, one thing has continued to astound me*: No one has any time, or more precisely – no one thinks they have any time.* And because they don't, the need to "cut to the chase" remains paramount. Speed rules – and along with it the desire for "tools and techniques." Now, I have nothing against tools and techniques. They can be very helpful. Golf pros give them out all the time. But tools and techniques are never enough – especially in the realm of innovation. Can they be useful? Yes, in the same way that jumper cables can be useful if your car won't start. *But first you need a car* – and after that, *someplace to go!* Without a car and a destination, jumper cables are just a meaningless prop.

If you are committed to birthing a Big Idea, first understand that the car is *you* and the engine that powers the car is your passion for bringing something new into the world. Only when *that* is in place will tools and techniques make any sense.

Some of the methods described on the pages that follow will be right up your alley. Some will not. Some are so common-sensical you'll think *you* could have invented them. Some are so *non-sensical* you'll dismiss them as trivial. Don't worry about loving them all. You won't. Just find the ones that capture your attention and give them a shot – whatever it takes to get those beautiful wheels inside you turning once again.

Two different parts of you will be activated by these methods: the *subconscious* and the *conscious*. The subconscious-activating tools will increase your receptivity to new ideas, helping you access the part of you that *already* knows. *This was Og's favorite approach.* Using the subconscious tools will feel a bit like walking into a dark room. At first there will seem to be nothing to see. But after a while your eyes will adjust and you'll begin making sense of what is already there.

The second set of tools is less about *receptivity* than *proactivity*. This approach presumes it is possible to quicken creativity by purposefully shaking things up. Experimentation is an important part of this approach – much in the same way that chemists mix and match elements in the hopes of synthesizing new discoveries.

Is there a perfect technique? No. Just like there's no perfect diet, place to live, or relationship. What works for you on Monday may not work for you on Sunday. What works for you in the morning may not work for you at night. But that's what makes the world – just like the wheel – go round and round. And that's why I offer you 35 different methods to choose from. Is there an organizing principle? Yes, there is. The tools fall into five categories:

1. **Attend:** To be present at; to take care of or wait upon; to listen and give heed to.

2. **Intend**: To have in mind as something to be done or brought about; to have a purpose or design.

3. **Suspend:** To defer opinion or evaluation to a later occasion; to render temporarily void.

4. **Extend:** To stretch out; to place at full length; to enlarge the scope of or make more comprehensive.

5. **Connect:** To join or unite; to establish communication between; to associate, attach, or place in relationship.

THE TOOLING UP TOOL BOX

1. ATTEND
- Write On! • Dream Catching • Happy Accident • Nature's Way • Embedded Reporter • Wiggy Bank • LCS

2. INTEND
- The Seed of Fascination • Get the Right Question • Dive In, Don't Come Up • Idea Brahmacharaya • Edison/Dali Method • Third Eye of the Storm • Silence of the Ams

3. SUSPEND
- Thought Experiments • Kidding Around • Lead Into Gold • The Good Thing About Bad Ideas • Opening the Flood Gates • Personas • Follow the Fallow

4. EXTEND
- Blue Sky Thinking • Act As If • The Daily Muse • Brainstorm • Strange Attractors • First Name Basis • Get a Move On

5. CONNECT
- The Idea Lottery • Patterns 'R Us • The Idea Buddy System • Metaphors Be With You • Build It! • Open Book Management • The Tool Machine

ATTEND

Creativity is free. Innate. Your birthright. But there is something you will have to pay for it and that is your *attention.* Or more specifically, your ability to be "mindful and aware." Mindful and aware of what? Ah! That is the question. Mindful and aware of what's going on *inside* you and *outside* you. Though all of us have five senses, we are not necessarily using them at all times. We look, but don't necessarily see. We listen, but don't necessarily hear. We reach out, but don't necessarily touch. Really creative people are doing all three – and then some. They are tuned in, alert, perceptive, and awake. They are in touch with the world inside them – and, more often than you might think, in touch with the world outside them, too. *What's going on inside?* Feelings, intuitions, notions, inklings, dreams, ideas, thoughts, memories, and impressions – the "stuff" from which true creativity springs.

What else do creative people attend to above and beyond their "selves?" The world *outside* them. The environment, society, culture, trends, patterns, people, the marketplace – and more specifically, *feedback* from potential users of the product or service they are creating.

Inside and outside. Both are essential. One without the other is like yin without yang. Lennon without McCartney. Your mother without your father. We need them both. Curiously, "creative types" have a tendency to overvalue what's on the *inside* while "business types" have a tendency to overvalue what's on the *outside.* The following seven tools will help you pay attention to both.

1. Write On!

Buddha, as the story goes, once said that human beings have 2,000 thoughts per second – and that he had slowed down his mind enough to be able to identify the last two. Few of us are in Buddha's league. Our thoughts are often a blur, flying in under the radar – great ideas mixed with odd bits about shoe sales, sex, and salad dressing. Like unremembered dreams, they come and go, having little or no effect on our lives. That's why we need a way to track them. At the very least, the effort to do so will give us the *option* of remembering them. Og recorded his ideas on the walls of his cave. You will also need a way.

What to Do:

• Keep an idea notebook with you at all times.

• When you get an idea that moves you, write it down.

• At least once a week, review your notebook.

> *NOTE: If a notebook isn't your style, find another medium: 3x5 index cards or a tape recorder. It doesn't matter what you use. The key is to capture your ideas before they fade away.*

2. Dream Catching

Many great breakthrough ideas have come in dreams. Rene Descartes got the concept for the Scientific Method in a dream. Elias Howe came up with the final design for the lock stitch sewing machine in a dream. August Kekule arrived at the formulation of the Benzene molecule in a dream. In the dream state, our subconscious mind arrives at solutions that our conscious mind is unlikely to discover no matter how much it obsesses. (That's why Thomas Edison and Salvadore Dali liked to take naps during the day.)

What to Do:

• Before you go to sleep tonight, bring to mind a question, challenge, or opportunity.

• As you fall asleep, stay focused on this topic.

• When you awake, write down your dream *even if the dream makes no sense to you.*

• Reflect on each element of the dream and see if you can make any connections to your Big Idea.

3. Happy Accident

A little known fact about innovation is how many breakthroughs have *not* been the result of genius, but "happy accidents" – those surprise moments when the answer revealed itself for no particular reason. The discovery of penicillin, for example, was the result of Alexander Fleming noting the formation of mold on the side of a petri dish left uncleaned overnight. Vulcanized Rubber was discovered in 1839 when Charles Goodyear accidentally dropped a lump of the polymer substance he was experimenting with onto his wife's cook stove. Breakthroughs aren't always about invention, but about the *inventiveness* required to notice something new, unexpected, and intriguing.

What to Do:

• Pretend you're a detective for the FBI ("Federal Bureau of Innovation").

• The next time anything goes wrong with a project of yours, stop and see if the seeming mistake offers any clues about new ways of proceeding.

4. Nature's Way

Leonardo DaVinci got his idea for the airplane by watching birds in flight. The creators of Kung Fu developed many of their techniques by watching animals fight. The pharmaceutical industry develops many of its "miracle cures" by studying the natural healing properties of herbs and plants. Bottom line, nature is a great source of breakthrough ideas. The secret for meeting your particular challenge, in fact, may have *already* been worked out thousands of years ago by a cockroach.

What to Do:

- Look to nature for clues about your challenge.
- Everywhere you walk today, notice how nature gets things done (i.e. bee hives, ants, sunflowers).
- Make a connection between the natural world and a still unresolved challenge of yours.

5. Embedded Reporter

There's a state of mind psychologists have dubbed the "hypnogogic state" that is a rich source of inspiration and fresh ideas. In this state, most often associated with the last few moments before sleep and the first few moments upon waking, the analytical mind is at bay and a fuzzier logic prevails. It is as if a portal opens between worlds and we gain greater access to the subconscious part of ourselves where brilliance often resides. Explained Victor Hugo, "There is visible labor, and there is an invisible labor." In the hypnogogic state, invisible labor rules the day.

What to Do:

• When you wake up tomorrow, don't get out of bed.

• Just lay there.

• Don't speak. Don't think. Don't move.

• Let thoughts, images, and feelings come to you.

• Surf them wherever they go. Then write them down.

6. *The Wiggy Bank*

Dr. Jonas Salk, the inventor of the polio vaccine, once said that "Intuition will tell the thinking mind where to look next." He knew, as do a lot of artists, actors, and entrepreneurs, that our *first* thought is often our *best* thought. "Beginner's mind," it has been called. "Gut instinct." The "hunch." Most of us, unfortunately, do not honor our first thoughts. Addicted to the linear world of logic and analysis, we usually ignore them.

What to Do:

• Buy a child's piggy bank and put it on your desk.

• Turn it into a "wiggy bank" by depositing, on small slips of paper, first thoughts as they come to you.

• At the end of the week, open your bank and study its contents.

• When you notice an intriguing idea, take a few minutes to develop it further or mention it to a friend.

7. *LCS*

Throughout history, the workplace has been host to many indoor sports: "Waste Paper Basketball," "Chair Racing," and "Inter-Office

Phony Phone Calls" are three of my favorites. But the biggest of them all, by far, has been "Idea Killing" – Big Business' answer to the World Wrestling Federation. The rules for this sport are so simple anyone can play: *Shoot down ideas as soon as you can, as fast as possible, by any means necessary.* Managers are quite good at this. As are CEOs, SVPs, and anyone else whose title can be abbreviated by a three-letter acronym. In fact, the higher up you go in an organization, the more skillful idea killing becomes. The real professionals don't even have to say anything. For them, a look is all it takes. During the past 20 years I've taught a lot of creative thinking techniques to people in the business world. One of these techniques has revealed itself to be the most powerful – a kind of Heimlich Manuever for anyone choking on doubt, negativity, or fear. It's called *LCS* – and it's especially powerful to use when others are trashing your idea before giving it a fair hearing.

What to Do:
- First, ask the naysayers what they *like* about your idea.
- Then, ask the naysayers for their *concerns* about your idea.
- Then, ask the naysayers for their *suggestions* in response to each of their concerns – ways to help you refine your idea.

NOTE: Ultimately, we are our own worse idea killers, which is the main reason why our ideas rarely see the light of day. In fact, we often kill our own ideas before any one else has a chance. Using the LCS method on your own fledgling ideas is a great way to ensure that at least some of them will get out of your head and into the world.

INTEND

If creativity is the flower of a human life, then *intention* is the root. Indeed, there are many people who believe that without intention, there can be no creativity. More than its second cousins – hope, wish, dream, and desire – intention is the ground from which creativity springs. One of the biggest reasons why creativity is so flaccid in most individuals (and by extension, most organizations) is that there is very little intention – and the intention that does exist is often a *simulation* of the real thing – upwardly mobile fast trackers inheriting someone else's vision, strategy, or idea but not sufficiently in touch with their own inspiration to really break through.

And so, if you want to create something new and meaningful, you will need to get in touch with your intention. *The force.* What moves you. Intention, of course, can take many forms. The intention to change. The intention to improve. The intention to serve. Whatever form it takes, your effort will need to be more than mental. More than emotional or psychological. It will need to be primal – in the same way that the moon affects the tides.

What is moving you? What is in your bones? What is your intention?

8. *The Seed of Fascination*

The reason why many of us do not get inspired ideas is because we are not inspired. The reason we are not inspired is because we do not follow our fascinations. The reason we do not follow our fascinations is because we judge them as impractical, irrelevant, or impossible. And so it goes, sometimes for an entire life. The good news? This cycle can be reversed. It begins by suspending judgment. It's followed by entertaining what fascinates you. It continues by getting inspired and then acting on the fruit of your inspiration.

What to Do:

- On a piece of paper, create three parallel headlines – the first, "What Fascinates Me," the second, "People I Admire," and the third, "What I Would Do If I Had More Time."
- Jot down at least five responses under each headline.
- Look for connections between your various responses.
- Write down your inspired ideas. Circle your favorite.

9. Get the Right Question

One of the biggest eye-openers for me as an innovation consultant is how rarely my clients understand what their real problems are. They may think they do, but they usually don't. Pressed for time, they rush from one meeting to the next (or one consultant to the next) trying to come up with solutions to problems that either don't exist or are not the *real* problem. Many ideas end up getting generated, but often in response to the *wrong* problem statement or, at the very least, a poorly articulated one.

What to Do:

- Write down your current challenge, starting with the words "How can I?" or "How can we?"
- Rewrite it at least *three* other ways.
- Circle the problem statement that feels the most accurate.
- Ask yourself if "there's a problem behind this problem" – a deeper issue that needs to be addressed.

- Show your new problem statement to a friend, get their feedback, and amend your question as needed.

10. Dive In, Don't Come Up

One of the reasons why Og was so successful with his Big Idea was because he *immersed* himself in the effort. Fascinated by the possibilities, he did everything he could to maintain his focus over time. And though he *did* get grief from Aargh and the rest of the tribe about removing himself from the demands of daily life, he succeeded in creating the kind of *sustained inner attention* almost always associated with a breakthrough. Perhaps, without email, a cell phone, and 500 cable channels to choose from, it was easier for Og to immerse than it is for us today. But still, we need to make the effort.

What to Do:

- Create four columns on a piece of paper and label them "Daily," "Weekly," "Monthly," and "Yearly."
- In each column, note what you can do in that particular time frame to immerse yourself in your most inspired venture.

11. Idea Bramacharaya

In India, spiritual adepts who give up sex to pursue God are known as "bramacharayas." They believe, as many Western spiritual practitioners do, that their vital power (i.e. kundalini) needs to be completely intact in order for them to have the ultimate experience. What does this have to do with *you*, oh sexually active seeker of the Big Idea? Plenty – especially when you consider that one of the main reasons why new ideas never see the light of day is because their originators "prematurely articulate." The act of *talking* about one's idea often takes the place of *doing* anything about it – and the idea, regrettably, ends up merely a fantasy.

What to Do:

• Nothing.

• If you get the urge to talk about your idea, don't.

• If someone asks you about your idea, thank them for asking, but explain it's too still too early to talk about it.

12. *The Edison/Dali Method*

As far as I know, Thomas Edison and Salvadore Dali never met. Nevertheless, they both were practitioners of the same creative thinking technique – one that is accessible to absolutely anyone with a chair. Realizing they got their best ideas upon waking, these two creative geniuses challenged the notion that a person had to wake only once a day. Instead, both men took periodic, idea-sparking naps. As the story goes, they would sit in a chair (not, as I mentioned, with each other), holding a coin or ball bearing in each hand, metal pie tin strategically placed below. When they nodded off to sleep, the object in their hand would fall, hitting the pie tin and waking them up. Immediately, they would jot down their thoughts, ideas, and insights.

What to Do:

• Find a chair, coin or marble, and two pie tins.

• Set up your napping area as noted in the above story.

- Take a nap.
- Upon waking, write down whatever is on your mind.

13. *Third Eye of the Storm*

At the center of every storm is total stillness. No matter how much swirling, flooding, and high winds may be happening on the periphery, at the core of every storm is complete quiet. The same holds true for the creative process. At the edges of your Big Idea, there is a great swirling: bills to pay, ovens to clean, cars to repair – the kind of stuff that can occupy all your time and attention. That is, *if* you let it. A true innovator will find a way to deal with the high winds and still have enough time to hatch their big idea – and they will do so in a way that does not judge the stuff on the seeming periphery to be any less important than the quiet at the center of the storm. In fact, if they judge, they will only end up creating more high winds and more stuff on the periphery they will have to deal with later.

What to Do:
- Make a list of your three biggest responsibilities.
- Create a plan for handling them.
- Whenever one of these responsibilities seems to trespass on the time you have to develop your Big Idea, close your eyes and take a few, deep breaths.
- Acknowledge the peripheral task that needs to be done and the person reminding you to do it.

• As you enter into the process of handling your responsibilities, remain at the center of the storm, continuing to concentrate on your breathing with the full realization that you will be returning to your "creative space" at just the right time.

14. Silence of the Ams

Do you know what the universe is made of? Not planets, comets, stars, or supernovas. Nope. Mostly empty space. Do you know what makes music interesting? Not the notes, but the pauses in *between* the notes. And in matters of love, do you know what makes the heart grow fonder? *Absence* – the spaces *in between* seeing one's beloved. For the innovator, it's the same way – or *could* be the same way – if only we paid more attention to the silence. In the silence exists the *receptivity* required to really *see* (and continue refining) the Big Idea.

What to Do:

• Be quiet for at least 30 minutes a day – more if possible.

• Consider this silence a "vacation." Do not try to *do* anything with it.

• In your silence, jot down any insights that come to you about your Big Idea.

SUSPEND

Perhaps Einstein said it best when he declared: "Not everything that can be counted counts; and not everything that counts can be counted." He was referring, of course, to the part of the human being that knows intuitively – the part of us that is tuned in, connected, and innately creative. Kids live in this place. The rest of us only visit, preferring the left-brained world of rationality, logic, linearity, practicality, and analysis. On some primal level, we're all from Missouri. We need proof. While there is nothing wrong with gathering data, the addiction to it subverts our ability to be creative. Somehow, we all know this. That's why we go to the movies, watch TV, read novels, and daydream. We seek an altered state, one that is free of the normal gravity of daily life. That's why brainstorm facilitators ask us to suspend judgment. That's why women, innately intuitive as they are, ask the men in their lives to stop being so damn practical and actually *feel* something for a change. It is in this state of suspension that our innate creativity is free to percolate to the surface – over, under, and around all of the left brained guardians at the gate.

And so… if you want to really birth a Big Idea, you too will need to enter into this state – at least in the first phases of your new venture. Suspend judgment. Suspend evaluation. Suspend your addiction to the practical. What exists on the other side is fuel for the fire of your untapped creativity.

What can you do this week to suspend practicality, logic, and rationality in service to birthing your Big Idea?

15. *Thought Experiments*

There is only one thing that's gotten a worse rap than dreaming. *Daydreaming.* Especially in the workplace. For most business people, daydreaming is the antithesis of working. Get caught daydreaming more than once on the job and you will quickly be labeled "unprofessional." And yet, daydreaming has been a powerful source of breakthrough ideas since the beginning of time. Albert Einstein, whenever he felt stuck, used to conduct what he called "thought experiments" (a fancy name for daydreaming) in his Princeton lab. And it was these flights of fancy, he claimed, that were often the catalyst for breakthrough.

What to Do:

• Take some time today to daydream.

• Follow your random, quirky thoughts with the same rigor you follow the stock market or office politics. Let your mind drift. Muse. Noodle. Reflect.

• If "business as usual," gets in your way, close your door or find another space to conduct your thought experiments.

16. *Kidding Around*

Some years ago, as the story goes, a large truck got stuck in a New York City tunnel. (Apparently the driver did not notice the maximum height sign.) Traffic backed up for miles while angry motorists waited impatiently for police and firemen to arrive. Just as the authorities were about to solve the problem by welding the top off the truck, a five year old girl, watching from the backseat of her parents' car, calmly asked why the grown ups didn't let some air out of the tires to lower the height of the truck so it could make it through the tunnel. Her father, tickled by his daughter's suggestion, got out of his car and passed on the idea to the powers that be. Problem solved.

What to Do:

• Pose your challenge to a child.

• Listen carefully to their range of responses.

• Even if no brilliant ideas emerge, look for the wisdom hidden within their most intriguing approach.

17. Lead Into Gold

One of the reasons why people don't innovate is because they are bound by limiting assumptions – those false conclusions and beliefs that tell us what is possible and what is not. (It's why lots of people never sailed to the "new world" and missed out on all that real estate. They assumed the Earth was flat.) Og's tribe also had a lot of assumptions, as did Og, himself. (So, by the way, did Fred Smith's college professor when he gave the future founder of FedEx a "C" on a paper describing the idea for an overnight package delivery service.) *Naming* the assumption, however, is only half the battle. The other half is finding a way to *transform* the assumption into a solution – much in the same way that alchemists, as legend goes, transformed lead into gold.

What to Do:

• Make a list of your assumptions about your Big Idea.

• Ask a friend or co-worker to add to your list.

- Turn each of your assumptions into a question, beginning with the words "How can I?"
- Choose the most intriguing question and brainstorm it.

18. The Good Thing About Bad Ideas

One of the inevitable things you will hear at a brainstorming session is something like: "There are no bad ideas." Well, guess what? There are *plenty* of bad ideas. Nazism, for instance. Arena Football. Bow ties. What well-meaning "keep hope alive" brainstorming aficionados really mean is this: Even bad ideas can lead to good ideas if the idea originator is committed enough to extract the meaning from the "bad." It happens all the time. Do you think *War and Peace* was written in one sitting? *Madame Butterfly? The Idiot's Guide to Volkswagen Repair?* No way. There were plenty of earlier drafts that were horrid, but eventually led to the final outcome. Even *diamonds* begin as *coal*.

What to Do:
- Bring your "How can I?" challenge to mind.
- Conjure up a really bad idea in response to this challenge.
- Write down anything good about this bad idea – an essence that is redeemable in some way.
- Using this redeemable essence as a trigger, generate at least three new ideas you *can* do something about.

19. Opening the Floodgates

Of all the constraints to creativity, perfectionism is the most devious. Posing as a high-minded ideal, it shuts down whatever innate, idea fluency abilities we may have. This phenomenon is especially troubling for people who work in organizations that subscribe to "quality improvement," Six Sigma, and other programs whose main focus seems to be reducing variability (i.e. mistakes). Hey, guess what? *Aspiring innovators need to make mistakes.* Mistakes are to innovation what experimentation is to science. Without the freedom to come up with some really awful ideas, it is highly unlikely you will ever come up with any good ones.

What to Do:

- Write down as many ideas as possible in the next five minutes in response to your most intriguing project.
- Do not censor yourself.
- Circle your favorite ideas.
- Choose one and brainstorm it for the next ten minutes.

20. Personas

Do you know why Halloween is such a popular holiday in America? People get permission to be *somebody else* for a night. Wearing a costume makes it easier to act differently, to let go of one's "normal self" – perhaps the simplest and most socially approved way to change perspective. And so, if *you* are feeling stuck or bound by old perceptions, why not declare today your own, personal Halloween? Try on a different mask. Be someone else for a change. The more you can look at your idea through the eyes of others, the easier it will be to have a creative breakthrough.

What to Do:

- Select a new persona – one of your heroes, perhaps.
- Close your eyes and imagine you *are* this new persona.
- Brainstorm your biggest challenge or opportunity through his/her eyes.
- Write down any new ideas you get about your project.

21. Follow the Fallow

When children are born prematurely, they are put in incubators until they are ready for the world. When fields stop producing, farmers let them lay fallow until the soil's nutrients are restored. It's the same with aspiring innovators. They too need to incubate. They, too, need to lay fallow – especially when they keep coming up empty. That's what Richard Wagner was doing just before the theme for Das Rheingold came to him as he stepped onto a bus. That's what Seymour Cray, inventor of the Cray supercomputer, used to do whenever he got stuck. Indeed, it's what *you* do every time you feel the need to "sleep on it" before making a decision. It's healthy. It's natural. It's a vital part of the creative process.

What to Do:

- Be aware if you are working hard, but not getting the results you want.
- If so, do something else for a change. Take a break.
- During this incubation phase, simply relax. If an idea comes to you during this time, write it down.

EXTEND

Usually, when a person has a creative breakthrough, there is an element of *stretching* involved – the effort to go beyond existing boundaries and extend into an unknown future. Surfers "hang ten." Astronauts "push the envelope." Ski jumpers lean far out over their skis. Most people don't want to extend very much because it's often uncomfortable, risky, and subject to the big, fat opinions of others. But rarely is there breakthrough without extension. Golfers use the expression "never up, never in" to describe what it takes to succeed with putting. Meaning? You have to putt the ball hard enough to have a chance of getting it into the hole. If you don't, you might get close, but close is all you'll get. Bottom line, if you want to break new ground, you will need to stretch. You will need to take some risks. You will need to extend beyond your normal ways of thinking and doing.

In what ways, this week, can you extend yourself beyond your normal limits in service to moving forward with your Big Idea?

22. Blue Sky Thinking

In 1989, Gary Kasparov, the Soviet Union Grand Chess Master, played a two game match against "Deep Blue," the reigning supercomputer of the time. Kasparov won easily. When asked by the media what his competitive advantage was, he cited two qualities: intuition and *the ability to fantasize*. (And this, from a master strategic thinker!) Few of us in the workplace are ever encouraged to fantasize – a behavior most commonly associated with children, flakes, or perverts. And yet, *fantasizing* is exactly how many breakthrough ideas get their start – the act of some maverick or dreamer entertaining the seemingly impossible.

What to Do:

- Make a *wish* for the successful resolution of your current challenge (i.e. "I wish I had more time").

- Extend this wish further by making a *wild wish* (i.e. "I wish I didn't have to work my regular job").

- Extend this wild wish even further by thinking of a *fantasy solution* – a seemingly impossible way to get a result (i.e. "A fairy godmother shows up at midnight to do my work").

- *Distill* your fantasy solution down to a core principle (i.e. "I get more help"…"I outsource my responsibilities").

- Using this core principle as a clue, brainstorm new ideas for the successful resolution of your challenge.

23. Act As If

Do you know what the opposite of a "*pro*fessional" is? A "*con*fessional." And, at the risk of being *un*professional, here is mine: One of the great secrets of the creative process is to *act as if* – to proceed in the spirit of *already* having succeeded – or if not having succeeded, then being merrily on your way to succeeding. Why is this so important? Because you already *are* what you profess to be, even if it's not apparent yet. This state of mind, which is the polar opposite of doubt, could easily be construed to be some kind of con game. It's not. In a con game, the intention is to deceive – to manipulate others by pretending to be something you're not. When you *act as if*, you are simply being that which you already are, but hasn't manifested yet. You are, as described in the introduction to this book, the *idea* of something not yet fully embodied. The intention is not to deceive, but to create a positive, life-affirming outcome. You are acting *confidently* (from the Latin *con-fide* – "with faith"), but are not playing a "confidence game."

What to Do:

• Suspend all doubt.

• See your Big Idea as already manifested.

• See yourself as the person whose Big Idea is already manifested.

• Start *acting as if* you are this person, quickly learning whatever you need to learn in order to close the gap between the *idea* of yourself and the full expression of this idea.

24. The Daily Muse

In the 21st century, it is no longer considered radical to believe that thought shapes the future. This is something that's been proven again and again in experiment after experiment. And it is precisely for this reason that the media has become such a powerful force in today's world. The media shapes thought. When we read something in a newspaper we assume it is true – and our lives begin to take shape around it. Well, here's your chance to take back the power of the press. And even more than that, here's your chance to *impress* your thoughts on the future – *your* future – and by extension, the rest of our futures *(so please be coming from the right place before continuing with this exercise).*

What to Do:

- Fast forward to a time in the future when you want your Big Idea to be fully manifested.
- Imagine you are a reporter from a prestigious newspaper, magazine, or blog.
- Write the story of your success, complete with testimonials, data, and anything else you care to add that will give your article *oomph.*

25. Brainstorm

Brainstorming is the act of joining together with others for the purpose of originating and developing new ideas. Unfortunately, brainstorming has become something of a con game in most organizations – a way that people in power officially foist their ideas on others or, at the very least, simulate the virtues they think their bosses will be measuring them against during the annual performance review charade. Fortunately, it doesn't have to be that way. With just a little bit of skill, structure, and the right mix of people you can return brainstorming to its proper seat in the pantheon of breakthrough thinking stimuli.

What to Do:

- Identify a "How can I?" question you care about.
- Invite 3-7 people to brainstorm this challenge with you.
- Make sure everyone understands the challenge.

- Communicate the following ground rules:
  - — Go for an abundance of ideas
  - — Be willing to suggest some wild ideas
  - — Listen and build on each other's ideas
  - — Withhold judgment
  - — Delay evaluation
- Capture all ideas on a flipchart.

26. Strange Attractors

Some years ago Sony had a policy that required its engineers to spend 25% of their time out of the office, mixing it up with people from other fields. Sony's management knew that new ideas often happen at the *intersections* between disciplines – not within the silos and turfs of like-minded people. This "strange attractors" phenomenon is why the Left Bank became so popular in France back in the 1940s. It was a fertile environment in which creative people could leave their individual turfs and become energized by others with different points of view.

What to Do:

- Pretend you are a reporter for your local newspaper.
- Go on a field trip that gets your juices flowing. If you work with others, take your team.
- Observe, listen, and take notes. Interview people that intrigue you.
- Read your notes within 24 hours, identifying at least one new insight or idea you can apply to your Big Idea.

27. First Name Basis

Conventional wisdom has it that the best time to name a new product or service is *after* you create it. *Unconventional* wisdom has it the other way around: *First you give your product or service a name, then you create it.* With this approach, the name – instead of being merely the descriptor of your creation – becomes the catalyst for its existence. The key is to come up with a compelling name – one that intrigues, entertains, or has embedded within it the kind of multiple meanings that stimulate you enough to decode them. Let's use the topic of this book – *creativity* – as an example. If I was looking to invent some new products to hawk in the back of the book, but had no clue what they were, I might start by generating some creativity-themed names – and then working backwards from there:

- *CreatiiviTeas:* Exotic teas that boost brainpower.
- *CreativiTees:* T-shirts featuring photos of famous creative people on the front and their inspired quotes on the back.
- *CreativiTease:* A card game that requires players to match famous quotes on creativity with the people who said them.

What to Do:

- Make up of a compelling name for something   even if you don't know what that "something" is. *Hint:* Humor, double entendre, and spelling variations are useful catalysts.
- Now that you have a compelling name of an imaginary product or service, brainstorm what that *something* might be.

28. Get a Move On

In addition to feta cheese, stoicism, and dancing on broken bits of glass at midnight, the Greeks have given us something else to marvel at: *The peripatetic school of education.* Founded by Socrates, this innovative approach to learning got students out of their heads by getting them out of the classroom. Socrates, like Og, literally "walked the talk," teaching as he strolled with his students. He knew, as Og did, that "When the body moves, the mind follows."

What to Do:

- The next time you feel stuck, admit it.
- Leave what you're doing and go for a walk.
- As you walk, notice what catches your attention.
- Make a connection between what catches your attention and your Big Idea.

CONNECT

True creativity rarely happens in a vacuum. On the contrary, it is the product of two or more variables connecting in new and interesting ways. It happens all the time in nature. Water, for example, is really just the connection between hydrogen and oxygen. So is hydrogen peroxide, but with a slightly different configuration. It happens in the human realm, as well. Roller blading is nothing more than the connection between ice skating and roller skating. MTV is nothing more than the connection between music and television. Drive-in banking? Car + banking, that's all. The originators of these breakthrough products and services didn't pull rabbits out of the air. All they did was see a useful, new connection between *already* existing elements – and then made the sustained effort to commercialize their newly conceived connection. Why don't more of us make these kinds of connections? Because we tend to stay with what we already know. We live in a box – whether that box is defined by our nationality, profession, concepts, cubicle, or astrological sign. The more we are willing to get out of this box – or, at the very least, see beyond it, the more likely it will be that powerful new connections will reveal themselves to us. If you want a breakthrough, it's time to start looking for new connections – uncommon linkages between this, that, and the other thing.

Who (or what) do you need to connect with in a new way in order to manifest your hottest, new idea?

29. *The Idea Lottery*

In 1939, a Russian immigrant owned the rights to distribute vodka in the U.S. His efforts bombed. Americans weren't attracted to a colorless, odorless alcohol. Depressed, he sold the rights to Heublein, an alcohol distribution company, who asked themselves a simple question: "What can we *combine* with Vodka to give it a distinctive color and a taste?" In time, they came up with tomato juice and, voila, the Bloody Mary was born, boosting sales of vodka through the roof. What most of us think of as innovation is really just the elegant combination of two (or more) pre-existing elements resulting in the creation of a new, value-added product or service. What is bungee jumping but the synthesis of jumping and rubber band? What was the Pet Rock, but the synthesis of rock and gift? Indeed, when Johannes Gutenberg was asked how he arrived at the invention of the printing press, he confessed it was as simple as seeing a new connection between two existing products: The wine press and the coin punch. If *you* are committed to coming up with a Big Idea, start looking for new connections between the stuff that's all around you.

What to Do:

- Create a 5x5 grid on a piece of paper.
- In 15 of the squares, write words that represent key elements of your current challenge (i.e. a person, place, task, process, or attitude).
- In the remaining 10 squares, write random words.
- Combine words in two or more squares and see if the relationship *between* those words spark any new ideas.
- Continue the process with other 2-word and 3-word combinations.

30. Patterns 'R Us

There are many people who make their living from the pattern recognition business: Futurists, meteorologists, air traffic controllers, and stock brokers just to name a few. And while their success rates may not always be 100%, it is clear that whatever success they enjoy is intimately tied to their ability to notice patterns and then interpret those patterns correctly for the rest of us. The same holds true for innovators. The only difference? Innovators, sometimes, hit the gravy train by *breaking* old pattern in new ways.

What to Do:

- Make a list of the patterns or trends associated with your Big Idea.
- Consider each of these patterns, one by one, and see if any new insights come to mind.
- Notice if there is a "pattern of patterns" and if so, what insights arise from those.
- Pick a pattern, then interpret it differently than most people would. Jot down any ideas that emerge.

31. The Idea Buddy System

Remember how Ugh's listening to Og was so helpful? But what about Og listening to Ugh? It never happened. Not once. Who knows what possibilities lurking within Ugh may have been fanned into flame if Og has been more *mutual* in his response. That's what the Idea Buddy System is all about. It's free, it's fun, and can be done over lunch with a minimum of muss and fuss.

What to Do:

- Identify someone whose support you want.
- Invite this person into a coaching partnership with you.
- Agree on the protocols and goals for your meetings.
- Choose a date, within the next week, and begin.

32. Metaphors Be With You

Since the beginning of time, the world's greatest teachers have used parable, fable, and metaphor to communicate their message. They knew that normal words alone would not suffice – that people needed a compelling image to consider, one that short-circuited the logical part of the brain and tapped directly into archetypal knowing. Metaphorically speaking, a metaphor builds a bridge between worlds. It allows the listener to be transported from one place (what they already know) to another (where the metaphor-maker is trying to take them). If you want to build a bridge from where you are now to where you want to go with your Big Idea, the next technique is for you.

What to Do:
- Create a metaphor that best describes what the *process* of manifesting your Big Idea feels like (i.e. Climbing Mt. Everest? Loading mercury with a pitchfork? Finding a needle in a haystack?)
- Describe the similarities (i.e. how the attempt to manifest your idea is similar to your metaphor).
- Brainstorm ways of overcoming each of the obstacles you just described.

33. Build It!

Do you remember one of Og's biggest boo boos at the beginning of his adventure? He forgot to give the tribe an example of what his invention looked like. All he showed them was a picture of a wheel, not the wheel itself. In his hurry to get buy-in, he forgot to make a prototype and along with it, one of the aspiring innovator's most important mantras: *If picture's worth a thousand words, a prototype is worth a million.* People need proof, especially skeptical, predominantly left-brained, rational, analytical, logical, number-crunching people. If they don't get it, they will eventually get *you.*

What to Do:

- Build a 3-D prototype of your idea.
- If you're not handy with building things, get help.
- Next time you pitch your idea to someone, bring your prototype along.

34. Open Book Management

While the so-called left brain thrives on law and order, the right brain thrives on serendipity, spontaneity, dislocation, and yes, even randomness. Indeed, many great creative breakthroughs owe their existence more to unexpected catalysts than they do labored thinking, analysis, or study.

What to Do:

- Contemplate your Big Idea for a minute or two.
- Open the nearest book, magazine, or newspaper.
- Close your eyes and place your finger on the page.
- Open your eyes and see what new insights come to mind when you make a connection between the word you're pointing to and the challenge you're working on.

35. The Tool Machine

Some years ago an architect designed an inner city housing project that received a lot of praise upon its completion. Residents of the project were thrilled to live there. Thrilled, but also confused. "You've forgotten to include *walkways,*" they complained to the architect at the ribbon cutting ceremony.

"Not at all," the architect replied, "that comes later – *after* I know where everyone walks." His strategy? To wait three months and pave over the pathways people naturally made by walking from building to building. The 34 previous tools and techniques in this book have been created in the same way. All I've really done is pave over creative pathways that work – based on 20 years of research and the facilitation of creative thinking sessions with more than 20,000 people in the business world. *That* and using my own curious self as a case study – observing my creative process… noticing where and when ideas came to me… putting myself under the microscope *and* the macroscope to see what worked, what didn't, and what *might*.

Which brings us to Tool #35 – a meta-tool to help you make your own tools. If you think I've left something out of this book, here's your chance to add it – to "round things out" as Og might say.

What to Do:

- Make a list of all the things you already do that help you originate, develop, and manifest new ideas.

- Select one idea-sparking behavior that intrigues you.

- Imagine that someone you love has never done such a thing and would benefit from doing so.

- Write step-by-step instructions that would enable this "someone you love" to emulate your behavior.

- Enter your creation into the *Awake at the Wheel Tools and Technique Contest* (see next page).

WRITING IT IN STONE

THE FIRST ANNUAL AWAKE AT THE WHEEL
TOOLS & TECHNIQUES CONTEST!

Tired of spending money on self-help books without much hope of getting a return on your investment? Relax. As Og's earthly representative, I am now authorized to accept entries into the *First Annual Awake at the Wheel Tools & Techniques Contest* – a simple way to make your money back and then some.

HERE'S HOW IT WORKS:

1. Follow the instructions for Tool #35.
2. Email your entry to:

    www.ideachampions.com/toolcontest.shtml

3. If your submission is selected for inclusion in the still-to-be-named *sequel* to this book, you win $100.
4. If your submission is voted the best reader-submitted tool to be published in the still-to-be-named sequel, you win $1,000. *Really.*
5. For more information, log onto:

    www.ideachampions.com/toolcontest.shtml

NEXTING: HOW TO INVENT THE FUTURE

I have no idea what Big Idea you worked on as you read this book. Maybe it was a way to cure cancer. Maybe it was a way to cure ham. The choice was yours. And your choice is none of my business. What *is* my business, however, is this: *Leaving the world a better place after I'm gone.* I mean, isn't that the idea – to go beyond our selves and really make a difference, whether that difference is experienced by a single individual or the entire planet?

Towards that end, I invite you now to pause for a moment and identify an even *bigger* idea than the one you've been noodling on as you read this book. Not just an idea that will help *you*, but an idea that will help *others* as well. This is not to say that your current Big Idea won't accomplish this noble goal. It might. All I'm suggesting is that there may be yet another way to be of service – something you haven't yet thought of. A something that would be of great help to your fellow Earthlings – the kind of something you might focus on if you were comfortably retired, independently wealthy, or just had a near death experience and suddenly more deeply appreciated the preciousness of life. Maybe it's an idea you've always wanted to develop, but didn't think you had the time…. or the money… or the support. Maybe it's a new idea sparked by this book. Whatever it is, now's the time to find out.

1.What are your three greatest gifts?

2.What is your biggest unfulfilled dream?

3.What does the world need more of?

4.What is your real work – not just your job?

5.What's one thing you want to create before you die?

STAYING ON A ROLL

RESOURCES FOR THINKING
OUTSIDE THE CAVE

Now that you're on a roll, it's a good idea to *stay* on a roll. Towards that end, I invite you to check out the resources below. Some are free. Some are not. But all of them will help you think outside the cave. *Wheely!*

WWW.IDEACHAMPIONS.COM: Inspiring articles on creativity and innovation. Includes *Idea Lottery*, *Jump Start* and *Free the Genie*, three interactive creative thinking tools, along with free downloads and the best FAQ on the web.

FREE THE GENIE: A deck of 55 brainstorming cards to help you bridge the gap between thought and action.
www.ideachampions.com/free_the_genie.shtml

IT'S AHAPPENING: A set of five creative thinking guidebooks to help you conjure up new ideas and solutions.
www.ideachampions.com/creative_thinking_guidebooks.shtml

INNOVATION KITS: A mixed bag of creative thinking tools, tips, and techniques. Something for both sides of your brain. www.ideachampions.com/innovation_kit.shtml

AWAKE AT THE WHEEL WEBSITE: Includes Mitch's speaking schedule, FAQs, inspiring quotes, and lots of other goodies. www.mitchditkoff.com

INGENUITY BANK: The next generation idea management software for your business or organization. A great way for your entire workforce to contribute their best thinking on a wide range of business challenges. www.ingenuitybank.com

BULK ORDERS OF AWAKE AT THE WHEEL: Hey, why keep this book all to yourself? Buy hundreds at a time and get a big break(through). www.ideachampions.com/aatw.bulkorder/shtml

OGCASTING:

Your Free Audio Bonus

Some people say a picture is worth a thousand words. Some people say a *cave painting* is worth a thousand words. Some people don't say anything, either because they're sleeping, watching TV, or dead. What do *I* say? *Me?* Og's earthly representative? I say an MP3 is worth a thousand pictures or, if not a thousand pictures, then at least ten minutes of your precious time. But not just *any* MP3. Nope. Uh uh. *The world's first OgCast.* That's right. Virtual Mitch emerging from his virtual cave to dive still deeper into the fabulous land of Big Ideas. Ten minutes to help you get out of your cave. Ten minutes to make this book come even more alive. Ten minutes to help you explore yet another way to stay awake at the wheel.

And I'm only just a click away.

WWW.IDEACHAMPIONS.COM/OGCAST.SHTML

ABOUT THE AUTHOR

Mitchell Lewis Ditkoff is the co-founder and President of Idea Champions, a management consulting and training company specializing in creative thinking, innovation, and team development. Educated at Lafayette College and Brown University, Mitch has worked with a wide variety of Fortune 500 and mid-sized companies who have realized the need to think (and do) something different in order to succeed in today's rapidly changing marketplace. These clients include: GE, Merck, Allianz, Lucent, NBC Universal, AT&T, Goodyear, Michelin, Pfizer, A&E Television Networks, General Mills, MTV Networks, Coca Cola, Infosys, Duke Corporate Education, Electronic Arts and a host of others. In addition to his corporate consulting work, Mitch is also an accomplished public speaker, poet, and baseball fanatic. Additionally, he is the founder of *Face the Music* (the world's first interactive business blues band) and co-creator of *Ingenuity Bank*, powerful, new idea management software that helps organizations streamline their process of originating, developing, and implementing new ideas. He lives in Woodstock, New York, with his wife, Evelyne (ageless), their two children, Jesse (13) and Mimi (10), and wonder dog, Chili (3). If you have an idea about what his next book should be, drop him an email today.

Contact: mitch@ideachampions.com

9 781600 372957